The 369 Manifestation Journal

A 52-Week Guide to Using Divine Numbers &
Law of Attraction Techniques to Manifest Your Desires

BERNI JOHNSON

ULYSSES PRESS

To my human and furry soul mates. I am grateful for you every day.

+ + +

Published by:
Ulysses Press
PO Box 3440
Berkeley, CA 94703
www.ulyssespress.com

ISBN: 978-1-64604-361-3
Library of Congress Control Number: 2022932319

Printed in China
10 9 8 7 6 5 4 3 2 1

Acquisitions editor: Kierra Sondereker
Managing editor: Claire Chun
Project editor: Renee Rutledge
Proofreader: Barbara Schultz
Front cover design: Raquel Castro
Interior design: what!design @ whatweb.com
Artwork: shutterstock.com
Layout and production: Yesenia Garcia-Lopez

Contents

Introduction to 369 Manifestation

The 369 Manifestation method is a ritual of setting goals and visualizing their attainment. It is an exercise in knowing what you want and directing your mind to get it. At its simplest, the method involves writing what you desire three times in the morning, six times in the afternoon, and nine times in the evening, with the ultimate goal of manifesting them in reality.

The 369 Manifestation method is a meld of the Law of Attraction—the idea that you attract what you put out into the universe, positive or negative—with a quote often (but likely erroneously) attributed to the vastly imaginative inventor Nikola Tesla (1856–1943): "If you only knew the magnificence of the 3, 6, and 9, then you would have the key to the universe." Ralph Bergstresser, author of *Dr. Nikola Tesla, The Forgotten Super Man of Our Industrial Age*, claimed he overheard Tesla say, "If you want to find the secrets of the universe, think in terms of energy, frequency, and vibration." This likely morphed into the 3-6-9 quote, which has been around for years but has reemerged on social media platforms like TikTok as users tout the efficacy of 369 Manifestation.

We know that Tesla was obsessed with the number three and numbers divisible by three. We also know that from the time he was a young child, he had a genius ability to visualize working inventions and bring them into being (a lesser-known fun fact is that his mother was an inventor of household gadgets). Tesla is best known for developing an efficient alternating current (AC) motor to generate electricity, a vast improvement over direct current (DC) and a feat that many thought impossible. He was also posthumously credited by the Supreme Court of the United States with the invention of the radio. Tesla's many other inventions and patents laid the foundation for today's technology. So it's not surprising that people would link him with manifestation. He demonstrated a form of it over and over.

You, too, can imagine what you want and bring it into being, starting now.

The Framework of This Journal

This journal begins with an introduction to the ideas behind 369 Manifestation, including visualization, creativity, gratefulness, mindfulness meditation, giving back to your community, and other useful New Thought techniques (see page 7). This will be followed by 52 weeks of inspirational quotes, exercises, and prompts to guide you through using the 369 Manifestation method.

With a framework for repeating and reinforcing your desires in life, this journal will help you plant the seeds to work toward your goals, consciously and unconsciously, in everything you do. You will learn how to craft affirmative statements, expressing what you want and harnessing the techniques to achieve your desires. Journal your way to positive thoughts, positive vibes, and positive outcomes. Let's get started.

Beginning Your Holistic Mindset Journey

All of the following ideas behind 369 Manifestation are good for both your mental and physical health and will help put you in the right mindset to achieve your desires.

Visualize Your Goals

Visualization is basically planning for a desired future outcome in your head. Imagining and then believing these goals are possible, and even inevitable, are important first steps toward manifesting them. Visualization has also been shown to decrease stress. Mental simulation of activities has been linked to better performance outcomes and improved skill in the likes of athletes and chess players. Some studies have even shown visualizing doing exercise can provide some of the benefits of the activity without the actual work!

There are different ways to visualize. You can close your eyes and picture attaining your desires in vivid detail. You can write your goals down, read over them, and imagine them as you are reading. You can create a vision board of images related to your desires to look at and regularly add to in order to stay focused on what you are working toward.

Our brains, by way of the thalamus, practice something called selective attention. So much information is thrown at our senses at every moment that the brain needs a way to prioritize, direct, and filter it down to what is important in the moment. As a result, a lot of this information gets tossed out. Visualizing your desires regularly can help keep your mind attentive to what you want and make it more likely that you'll perceive things that could help you attain your goals, such as job, networking, or learning opportunities.

However you choose to envision what you want to materialize, do so as if you have already achieved or gained them, and in as much detail as possible, bringing as many of your senses as possible into the vision. Place yourself in the visualization and imagine how the setting of this achievement looks, sounds, smells, tastes, and feels. Let the positive emotions associated with it wash over you.

Attract Your Desires

The Law of Attraction is an idea that sprang out of the New Thought movement in the 1800s and early 1900s—a movement that melded spirituality and psychology and touted the power of positive thinking in healing and achieving other beneficial outcomes. The law was expounded upon in Charles F. Haanel's 1912 twenty-four-week correspondence course, later released as a book called *The Master Key System*. Rhonda Byrne's 2006 book *The Secret* repopularized the concept.

At its simplest, the Law of Attraction is that you attract whatever you think about. Positive thoughts lead to positive things coming your way, and negative thoughts lead to negative things coming your way.

Although it sounds like magical thinking or spiritualism, the original idea as explained by Haanel revolved around the conscious and unconscious (or subconscious) minds. According to Haanel, the conscious mind feeds thoughts and ideas to your subconscious mind, which works in the background to perform the miracles that get you what you want.

There is something to the idea that our subconscious minds work in our favor, or sometimes, disfavor. Have you ever done or said something that seemed to come out of nowhere? Have you sabotaged yourself and later wondered why? Or have you come up with a brilliant idea upon waking, for a project you'd been working on the previous day? Our unconscious minds work continuously (and without our direct supervision) in ways we do not yet fully understand.

Proponents of the Law of Attraction credit it with the ability to generate health, wealth, and happiness. Although you shouldn't rely on your mind alone if you receive a serious medical diagnosis—modern medicine has done a lot to increase our lifespans and improve quality of life—there is a phenomenon called the placebo effect, where a doctor gives a patient a fake remedy (sometimes a sugar pill) and says it will help with a symptom. A percentage of patients will experience the supposed positive effect of the placebo even though it contains no medicine. They think the placebo works, so it does.

The Law of Attraction in the context of 369 Manifestation doesn't mean you write "I will have a giant mansion" over and over, and your dream house will magically appear. The idea is that by writing out your wants and focusing on them repeatedly, your mind will help you work toward that ultimate goal, steering you where you need to be and toward the decisions you need to make to achieve your dreams. All this positive thinking also helps you in other ways.

Benefit from Positivity

People who dwell in and focus on positive thoughts are likely to have better physical and mental health and are more likely to attain their goals. Positive thinking and dispositional optimism have also been linked in studies to lower risk of heart disease, decreased anxiety and depression, higher pain tolerance, better health outcomes when recovering from surgery, and even longer life span—which at the very least could give you more time to achieve your dreams.

Optimists tend to be problem-solvers, which can help them overcome obstacles on the path to success. They are less likely to wallow in the negative and are therefore quicker to spring back into action after setbacks. Pessimists are more likely to avoid their problems, and optimists are more likely to face them. It's easy to see which you should strive to be.

Although a total personality change isn't likely, or even warranted, there are things you can do to increase your positivity.

Practice Gratefulness

One positivity booster is regularly expressing gratitude for what you already have. Practicing gratefulness has been linked to better mental health. Benefits include decreased depression and stress, fewer harmful emotions like envy and regret, reduced chance of burnout, increased happiness, increased optimism, increased self-esteem, and increased empathy, patience, and humility—things that can help improve your interpersonal relationships, which have also been linked to better health outcomes throughout life.

In addition, expressing gratitude has been shown to reduce aches and pains, decrease fatigue, increase the frequency of exercise, increase the likelihood of regular doctor's visits, and improve sleep—all things that contribute to better health in general. Gratitude journaling has even been linked with decreased bodily inflammation.

So, while working toward your goals with the 369 method, make sure to express gratitude for what you currently have. On a daily or weekly basis, pick at least three things for which you are thankful. You can write them down in the gratitude exercises provided later in this journal, say them out loud, or think them to yourself. You can even express gratitude directly to the people for whom you are grateful, which might even help to boost their positivity and gratitude.

Magic of Numbers Divisible by 3

There are cool things about all numbers divisible by 3. For one, if you want to know if a number, no matter how long, is evenly divisible by 3, add the digits of the number recursively until you get down to a single digit number. That number will be either 3, 6, or 9 (the single-digit numbers divisible by 3). For instance, the digits of 1,279,362 add up to 30, 3 + 0 equals 3, and 1,279,362 is evenly divisible by 3.

There is also potential "magic" in the repetition of ideas and statements. While the exact numbers may not be important, the 369 method takes advantage of repetition. Repeating thoughts or statements helps drill them into your brain. Negative repetitious thoughts, like worry and self-reproach, have been linked to negative health effects, such as depression, suppressed immune response, and heart disease. But positive repetitious thought, such as reminiscing about, savoring, or anticipating good things, has been linked to more positive outcomes, such as reduced stress and depression, overall psychological well-being, better cognitive health, and better physical health.

Repetition also reinforces the ideas you want to foster in yourself. Our thoughts have some bearing on which neural pathways are strengthened in our brains. We are learning more and more about neuroplasticity, the ability of the brain and its pathways to change, and about our ability to drive that change.

Reiterate what you want your mind to work toward. Use the power of repetition by writing your powerful, positive, present-tense or future-tense statements 3, 6, and 9 times each day.

Take Positive Action

There is no attraction without action. Well, there might be if you're very lucky, but most of the time you have to put in some effort through positive, constructive action. Repeated wants and affirmations help get you into the right mindset to act on your goals and set your unconscious to the task of figuring out what actions are required and what opportunities to seize.

The act of figuring out your goals is, in fact, one action you can take. Writing them down is another. The first week's exercise in this book prompts you to do both. This journal will help you come up with other small steps to work toward what you want throughout your journey.

Discover What You Want

To focus on what you want to manifest, you must first know what you want. You must determine your specific goals to journal them and set your mind on the path toward your dreams.

Figuring out what you really want out of life requires some self-reflection. Ask yourself what you would be doing if you didn't have to worry about the obstacles outside of yourself that are standing in your way (such as money, time, or relationship dynamics). Think about what you would like to achieve and what you feel you need to do so. Ask what makes you happy and what you would like to bring more of into your life.

But also ask yourself what makes you unhappy or brings you displeasure. Reflecting on what you don't like or enjoy can be reverse-engineered to help you figure out what you can change or achieve to mitigate the unfavorable— to shine a light on what you actually want.

Formulate and write down clear and specific wants. And if, in the course of life, you decide you desire something different from what you initially thought you wanted, reformulate and write down your new motives. They don't have to be static. Circumstances and feelings change. Pick your current goals, and the next step is believing that you can achieve them. The approaches detailed in the pages to follow can help you on your way.

Foster Creativity

Contrary to popular belief, creativity is not something some people have and some people don't. And you aren't born with a finite amount. You can foster and improve your creative capabilities through a variety of means, including physical exercise, relaxation techniques, reading, writing, art, music, study, and travel, among other things. New stimuli breed new thoughts and connections that spur your imagination.

Creativity is an important factor in innovation and problem-solving. And it's obviously essential to artistic endeavors, if that's where your passions lie. But it has also been identified as a predictor of longer lifespan. After all, creativity is why we have been so capable of adapting and thriving as a species. So, feed your mind and take part in creative exercises and endeavors as often as you can.

Practice Self-Compassion

Self-compassion, or self-kindness, is important to our mental health and ability to achieve our desires. Harsh self-criticism has been shown to increase anxiety, reduce happiness, and even lead to procrastination. Dwelling on mistakes does little good. It's better to realize that you—like everyone else—are human. We all make mistakes. Learn from them, but don't beat yourself up about them repeatedly. Remember, repetition can be used for bad or for good. Forgive yourself and move on.

Self-compassion has been shown to reduce stress and anguish-induced inflammation, and to reduce instances of other physical health problems like headache and back pain. People who practice self-kindness are more mentally resilient and more likely to take action to correct mistakes, giving them a higher likelihood of success at achieving their desired goals (Robson 2021).

Explore Mindfulness Meditation

More and more, the medical community is recognizing meditation as a benefit to mental and physical health. The practice has been linked to increases in creativity, energy, and feelings of happiness, and to reductions in anxiety, pain, high blood pressure, and cholesterol. A Harvard study demonstrated that meditation could result in rebuilding parts of your brain, including increasing gray matter density in areas associated with memory, learning, compassion, introspection, and self-awareness, and decreasing gray matter density in an area associated with stress and anxiety (McGreevey 2011; Riopel 2021b). These changes can lead to better cognition and less anxiety. Other researchers found that mindfulness meditation can lengthen the telomeres that protect our DNA (the shortening of which is associated with aging) (Alidina 2020).

There are many types of meditation. One is transcendental meditation, a practice rooted in Indian Vedic tradition where the meditator sits silently, eyes closed, and thinks a mantra over and over. Learning this method involves guidance from a certified instructor over multiple sessions. Mindfulness meditation is another popular type, with many subtypes, that is easier to learn on your own and start practicing quickly.

In mindfulness meditation, you bring your focus to the present, usually by paying attention to your breathing, bodily sensations, emotions, thoughts, or other images around you while you are meditating. If your mind wanders away from what you are trying to focus on, the aim is to acknowledge and then dismiss the intrusive thoughts without judging them or yourself, and to bring your focus back to the moment. You can perform mindfulness meditation in a comfortable meditation pose for a set period of time or while you are doing your normal daily activities.

This journal includes several mindfulness meditation exercises to potentially help you on your journey. You can also find guided meditations online (via video, podcasts, or apps) that give step-by-step instructions on things like how to breathe and what to focus on. If you are so inclined, feel free to delve into other categories of meditation to see if they are for you. Everyone is different. Finding whatever works for you is key.

Get Moving

It's important to exercise your body as well as your mind. Physical activity has both physical and mental health benefits, including decreased anxiety and improvements in mood and self-esteem. Exercise can also improve your sleep, and better sleep is likewise beneficial to body and mind. And exercise boosts energy, which can help you work toward your goals.

Even simply walking gets your blood pumping and feeds more oxygen to your brain. Exercise has been demonstrated to immediately improve attention and memory. Over time, it also helps prevent age-related brain tissue deterioration and helps build new brain connections.

What's good for your brain is good for your ability to manifest your desires, so add in some regular physical activity. It doesn't have to be a lot, or very strenuous. Get moving in whatever way you are able—and preferably in a manner that you enjoy—for a few minutes a day.

Give Back

Manifestation can sound like taking what you want without giving anything. But in his Master Key program, Charles Haanel stressed that you should also focus on being of service to others in a way that everyone benefits. In other words, don't lie, cheat, and steal your way to good fortune. Be honest and fair in your dealings.

Giving back is obviously the right thing to do, but it's also good for you! Studies have linked altruistic behavior, like giving gifts, donating to charity, volunteering, and helping others, with increased happiness, reduced stress, lower blood pressure, and greater longevity. Doing things for other people takes our focus from ourselves and makes us feel better. It also fosters social connections and inspires others to be generous, sometimes to you. So giving to others is giving to yourself—a win-win!

Now that you have a little more information on the benefits of 369 Manifestation and the practices that complement it, it is time to begin.

This journal includes lines for one set of the 3, 6, and 9 goal affirmations per week. To reinforce them on the other days of the week, either think, read aloud, or write each statement on your own paper 3 times in the morning, 6 times in the afternoon, and 9 times in the evening.

Week 1

Discover What You Want

"By recording your dreams and goals on paper, you set in motion the process of becoming the person you most want to be. Put your future in good hands—your own."

— **Mark Victor Hansen, founder of**
***Chicken Soup for the Soul* series**

Exercise A: List some of the things you want to attain or bring into your life. Be as specific as you can. What would give you your dream life?

....

....

....

....

If you had any trouble formulating this list, don't panic! A helpful exercise in figuring out what you truly desire is brainstorming the things you don't like about your life and using that to come up with goals that would improve your situation. Are there things you dislike about your job, your relationships, or your lot in life? List them, and then work out some positive counters with the following exercise.

Exercise B: List your dislikes on the left. Then, to the right of each, write what you would like to have, be, or do instead.

What I dislike about my life	What I would like instead

Exercise C: Convert the wants from the right-hand column into specific statements of what you want to manifest in your life. Create positive, present-tense statements as if you already have a particular commodity or career, perhaps starting with "I have" or "I am." For instance, "I am a successful writer," although it can be more detailed and specific than that. If present-tense sounds too odd to you for your particular goal, feel free to switch to future tense. For instance, for a material desire, like gaining money, "I will attain a million dollars" might sound better to you than "I have a million dollars." Go with what resonates best with you.

....

....

....

....

....

Pick one goal you want to focus on manifesting. Once you have your chosen statement, you are ready to begin repeating your desire, starting in the morning. As you write your manifestation statement, practice visualization by picturing yourself already having achieved the stated goal, and savor the positive emotions this accomplishment gives you.

369 Manifestations

In the morning, write what you want to manifest 3 times.

1. ....

2. ....

3. ....

In the afternoon, repeat what you want 6 times.

1. ....

2. ....

3. ....

4. ....

5. ....

6. ....

In the evening, reinforce your desires 9 times.

1. ....

2. ....

3. ....

4. ....

5. ....

6. ....

7. ....

8. ....

9. ....

There is one set of the 3, 6, and 9 goal affirmations per week in the journal. To reinforce them on the other days of the week, either think, read aloud, or write each statement on your own paper 3 times in the morning, 6 times in the afternoon, and 9 times in the evening.

Week 2

Build Yourself Up

"Believe you can and you're halfway there."
— **Theodore Roosevelt**

Negative thoughts and negative self-talk can diminish your sense of well-being and self-confidence. Drive them away with positive affirmations.

Build yourself up. Make yourself believe that you can achieve your aims. And whenever a negative thought intrudes on your well-being, try to spin it into a positive affirmation. For example, if your goal is to pass an exam and you are having doubts about your intelligence or your ability to learn, positive statements like, "I am an intelligent human being" and "I am a quick learner" turn those negative thoughts around.

Exercise: Write several positive affirmations, such as "I am worthy of love," "I have wonderful and loving friends," or "I am a capable human being." Although general positive affirmations are beneficial, feel free to add more detail, and to relate them to your 369 Manifestation statements. For instance, if this week's manifestation statement is about passing that exam, try to make at least one of your affirmations about your abilities in that area. Once you have written out each of your affirmations once, either rewrite them several times each or repeat them aloud several times. You may even wish to speak them into a mirror or say them while exercising.

I am...

I have...

369 Manifestations

In the morning, write what you want to manifest 3 times.

1. ....

2. ....

3. ....

In the afternoon, repeat what you want 6 times.

1. ....

2. ....

3. ....

4. ....

5. ....

6. ....

In the evening, reinforce your desires 9 times.

1. ....

2. ....

3. ....

4. ....

5. ....

6. ....

7. ....

8. ....

9. ....

Week 3

Brainstorm Positive Action

"Imagination is the beginning of creation. You imagine what you desire, you will what you imagine, and at last, you create what you will."

—George Bernard Shaw

You are journaling statements to focus your brain on what you want and get your mind in gear to achieve it. But to make progress, you have to take actions toward achieving your goals. You must play a game if you want to win it. You must train to be a successful athlete. You usually must apply for a job in order to get it (although you may be lucky enough for networking to play a role there, too).

To achieve our loftier aims, it helps to break them down into smaller tasks. Brainstorm positive actions you can take to get you closer to your goal. They can be baby steps. For a job change, this could look like updating your resume, then sending it out to places you might want to work. You can take a class (online or in person), watch a tutorial, or read a book to teach yourself something new. You can practice a skill you already possess to become even better at it. If your goal is to write a book, you could resolve to write a little every day—even just a single line. As the old adage goes, every journey begins with a single step.

Exercise: Brainstorm possible actions that relate to your chosen manifestation and write them out below. Commit to at least one in the next week.

....

....

....

....

....

....

....

....

369 Manifestations

In the morning, write what you want to manifest 3 times.

1. ....

2. ....

3. ....

In the afternoon, repeat what you want 6 times.

1. ....

2. ....

3. ....

4. ....

5. ....

6. ....

In the evening, reinforce your desires 9 times.

1. ....

2. ....

3. ....

4. ....

5. ....

6. ....

7. ....

8. ....

9. ....

Week 4

Be Grateful

"Once we believe in ourselves, we can risk curiosity, wonder, spontaneous delight, or any experience that reveals the human spirit."

—E.E. Cummings

Stopping to think about and express what you are grateful for in life has benefits, including stress reduction and helping you cope with everything life is throwing at you. Reflect on good things that have happened in the recent past—things that you are proud to have accomplished or are thankful to have.

Did you nail a project at work? Did a social interaction go particularly well? Do you have people (or pets) you love in your life? Have you taken any measures to improve or maintain your health? Have you survived a global pandemic?

Exercise: Write down at least three things you are grateful for right now. If you can think of more than three, fill in all the space you want, or grab a notepad and write away! And feel free to tie them in with this week's manifestation statement by including gratitude for any steps you've made toward your goals.

I'm grateful for

....

....

....

....

I'm grateful for

....

....

....

....

I'm grateful for

....

....

....

....

....

....

....

....

369 Manifestations

In the morning, write what you want to manifest 3 times.

1. ....

2. ....

3. ....

In the afternoon, repeat what you want 6 times.

1. ....

2. ....

3. ....

4. ....

5. ....

6. ....

In the evening, reinforce your desires 9 times.

1. ....

2. ....

3. ....

4. ....

5. ....

6. ....

7. ....

8. ....

9. ....

....

Week 5

Visualize Your Dreams

"Visualization is daydreaming with a purpose."

—Bo Bennett, author and founder of eBookIt.com

Visualizing is one way to keep your mind focused on what you want to manifest in your life. Use your mind's eye to see yourself with your desires already attained. What do your surroundings look like? What sounds do you hear? What do your clothes and other items around you feel like? Are there any pleasant smells or tastes associated with your goals? Is there chocolate?

Take a few minutes, preferably daily, to imagine yourself having what you want to have and doing what you want to do.

Exercise: Close your eyes and imagine yourself living your dream life, having already achieved your goals. If your aim is to become an athlete or an artist, for example, you can picture yourself scoring a goal in a sold-out stadium or greeting loved ones at a gallery opening. Put yourself into a scene (preferably related to this week's manifestation statement) and fill it with satisfying sights, soothing sounds, nice aromas, delicious tastes, and rich textures. Afterward, write down (or even draw) the scene in as much detail as possible and use it as a jumping-off point for daily visualization.

369 Manifestations

In the morning, write what you want to manifest 3 times.

1.
2.
3.

In the afternoon, repeat what you want 6 times.

1.
2.
3.
4.
5.
6.

In the evening, reinforce your desires 9 times.

1.
2.
3.
4.
5.
6.
7.
8.
9.

Week 6

Feed Your Creativity

"Your imagination is everything. It is the preview of life's coming attractions."

—Albert Einstein

Our imaginations allow us to envision the future, think through problems before they arise, and come up with innovative ideas that can be turned into reality. You should stimulate your creativity regularly. Fortunately, there are lots of ways to do this, including (but not limited to) meditation, exercise, taking in new scenery, reading fiction, and even doodling.

Exercise: Spend a few minutes doodling whatever springs to mind in the space on the next page. Feel free to draw (or even color) outside the margins. Try patterns, shapes, simple objects, complex structures, clothing, people, pets, new creatures, scenery—the sky's the limit. On second thought, there is no limit. You can draw outer space, too! And feel free to spend the last minute or so doing quick sketches of images your weekly manifestation statement brings to mind.

369 Manifestations

In the morning, write what you want to manifest 3 times.

1. ....

2. ....

3. ....

In the afternoon, repeat what you want 6 times.

1. ....

2. ....

3. ....

4. ....

5. ....

6. ....

In the evening, reinforce your desires 9 times.

1. ....

2. ....

3. ....

4. ....

5. ....

6. ....

7. ....

8. ....

9. ....

Week 7

Visualize Your Accomplishments

"You must expect great things of yourself before you can do them."

—Michael Jordan

Belief in yourself is a key component to achieving your dreams. There will be people who love and support you, but on the flip side there will be those who naysay everything you do or want to do. Believing in yourself makes it easier to dismiss the negative voices around you and keep them from derailing you—or keep you from derailing yourself on their behalf.

One useful exercise in pumping up your belief in yourself is to think about things you've already accomplished. Look around you at what you have (materially and otherwise), at your relationships with loved ones (including pets), at tasks you've nailed—anything that you've done or gained during your lifetime. These successes can be from work, school, leisure time, or life in general, from your earliest memories to your latest. Pick one you are particularly proud of, or that makes you happy, and do a visualization exercise that starts in your past and moves forward into your future. Remember, you've reached desired goals before. You can do it again!

Exercise: Close your eyes and picture your chosen past acquisition, achievement, or performance. Put yourself into the scene and fill it with related sights, sounds, aromas, tastes, and textures. Notice the feelings of joy or gratification the visualization engenders. After luxuriating in the fond memories, switch to visualizing your new desire, and associate the same positive thoughts and feelings with what you want to manifest. Afterward, jot down (or doodle) any thoughts or feelings—or even new ideas—this exercise brings to the surface.

369 Manifestations

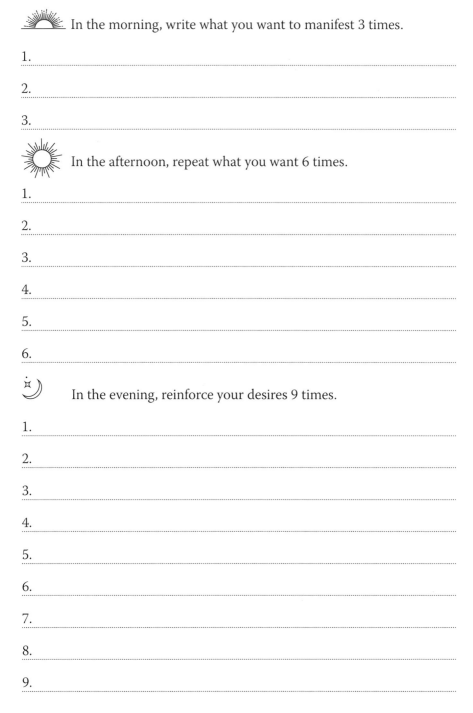 In the morning, write what you want to manifest 3 times.

1.

2.

3.

 In the afternoon, repeat what you want 6 times.

1.

2.

3.

4.

5.

6.

 In the evening, reinforce your desires 9 times.

1.

2.

3.

4.

5.

6.

7.

8.

9.

Week 8

Breathe

"If you know the art of deep breathing, you have the strength, wisdom, and courage of ten tigers."

—Chinese adage

Stress has been linked to medical issues like high blood pressure and a suppressed immune system, as well as mental health issues like anxiety and depression. Relaxation can help alleviate these issues, and one way to invoke your body's relaxation response is by practicing breathing exercises. In fact, breathing deeply is a component of other practices known for their relaxation benefits, such as meditation and yoga. Breathe in, breathe out, and relax.

Exercise: Sit or lie in a comfortable position. Take a slow deep breath through your nose (a few seconds long), allowing your chest and belly to expand. Exhale just as slowly through your mouth or nose. Repeat ten or more times. Write how you feel. Try this any time you feel stressed. You might also want to do so before choosing or writing this week's manifestation statement.

....

....

....

....

....

....

....

369 Manifestations

In the morning, write what you want to manifest 3 times.

1.

2.

3.

In the afternoon, repeat what you want 6 times.

1.

2.

3.

4.

5.

6.

In the evening, reinforce your desires 9 times.

1.

2.

3.

4.

5.

6.

7.

8.

9.

Week 9

15 Minutes of Movement

"Walking is a man's best medicine."

—Hippocrates

We've done lots of mental and written exercises in this journal, but another useful tool for improving the mind and spurring the imagination is actual exercise—the physical kind. Physical activity can reduce anxiety, improve mood and self-esteem, increase memory and attention, improve sleep quality, and boost energy, all of which can be an advantage to working toward your desires.

So this week's exercise is exercise itself! All the better if you can make it a daily (or near-daily) habit, even if you only have a few minutes to spare.

Exercise: Go for a walk for fifteen minutes. If you don't like walking, pick another activity of your choice. You can stretch, do calisthenics, dance around the house to music, jump rope, do yoga, or anything else you enjoy. Bonus points for thinking about this week's desired 369 Manifestation goals while moving around. Afterward, jot down any related ideas that came to mind during or just after the physical activity.

....

....

....

....

....

....

....

....

369 Manifestations

In the morning, write what you want to manifest 3 times.

1. ....

2. ....

3. ....

In the afternoon, repeat what you want 6 times.

1. ....

2. ....

3. ....

4. ....

5. ....

6. ....

In the evening, reinforce your desires 9 times.

1. ....

2. ....

3. ....

4. ....

5. ....

6. ....

7. ....

8. ....

9. ....

Week 10

Question Negative Thoughts

"If you don't like something, change it. If you can't change it, change your attitude."

—Maya Angelou

Our attitudes have a huge effect on how we act, how we feel, and our general enjoyment of life. Negative self-talk can keep us from feeling confident enough to move ahead. Fortunately, our outlook is something we can change. And one way is by interrogating negative thoughts.

Socratic questioning is a technique named for the ancient Greek philosopher Socrates, who was known to undertake dialogue with his students through questioning rather than simply lecturing them. The method is used in cognitive behavioral therapy and consists of asking and answering questions about a thought to come at it from different angles. The aim is to help patients reframe irrational thoughts. When a negative thought is causing you stress, deflating your self-esteem, or otherwise plaguing you, try Socratic questioning to defang the thought.

Exercise: Write down a thought that is nagging you (preferably one you think could keep you from achieving your desired manifestation) and answer three or more of the following questions about it.

Thought:

1. What evidence backs up this thought? What evidence refutes it?

2. What assumptions am I making?

3. Are there other possible points of view? If so, what are they?

4. Is this thought based on feelings or facts?

5. Is the thought black and white, or does it represent the complexities of reality?

6. What led me to think this thought? Have I always thought it?

....

....

7. If the thought were true, what would the consequences be?

....

....

After questioning your thought, do you see it a different way? Is it less scary? If you determined it is true, can you now think of ways to work around it? Write out a new, more positive version of the original thought and, if applicable, any solutions that spring to mind:

....

....

....

....

....

....

....

....

....

....

....

369 Manifestations

In the morning, write what you want to manifest 3 times.

1.

2.

3.

In the afternoon, repeat what you want 6 times.

1.

2.

3.

4.

5.

6.

In the evening, reinforce your desires 9 times.

1.

2.

3.

4.

5.

6.

7.

8.

9.

Week 11

Acknowledge Your Achievements

"Trust yourself. You know more than you think you do."

—Dr. Benjamin Spock

Most people tend to belittle themselves too much. But you are a fount of knowledge and a beacon of accomplishment. Have you learned a skill? Studied any topics that interest you? Had a positive impact on others? Helped a friend with a problem? Expressed love or appreciation to anyone? We all have things we are good at and things we have accomplished. It's time to acknowledge some of yours.

Exercise: Brainstorm examples of your skills, knowledge, accomplishments, good deeds, etc. Include anything from small acts of kindness to completed projects. Just getting out of bed and facing the day can be an accomplishment. And you've done that lots of times! What else have you done? Build up your self-esteem, and when you repeat your manifestation goals, believe that you can do it.

369 Manifestations

In the morning, write what you want to manifest 3 times.

1.

2.

3.

In the afternoon, repeat what you want 6 times.

1.

2.

3.

4.

5.

6.

In the evening, reinforce your desires 9 times.

1.

2.

3.

4.

5.

6.

7.

8.

9.

Week 12

Practice Self-Compassion

"You yourself, as much as anyone in the entire universe, deserve your love and affection."

—Buddha

You are both worthy and capable of kindness, and the first person to whom you should show it is yourself. When you make mistakes or missteps or do something embarrassing, don't beat yourself up. These self-conscious mental beatings can take a toll and hold you back. Forgive yourself. You are human. Tell yourself that everyone stumbles. And most mistakes and failures come with lessons that help you make better decisions in the future. Live, learn, and move forward.

Exercise: List several things you consider mistakes from your past. Then write down what lessons they taught you. Finish up with a statement of self-forgiveness for all bygone regrets. Let them go and resolve to learn from them rather than berating yourself. You will be better off for showing yourself compassion and better able to tackle your manifestation goals.

369 Manifestations

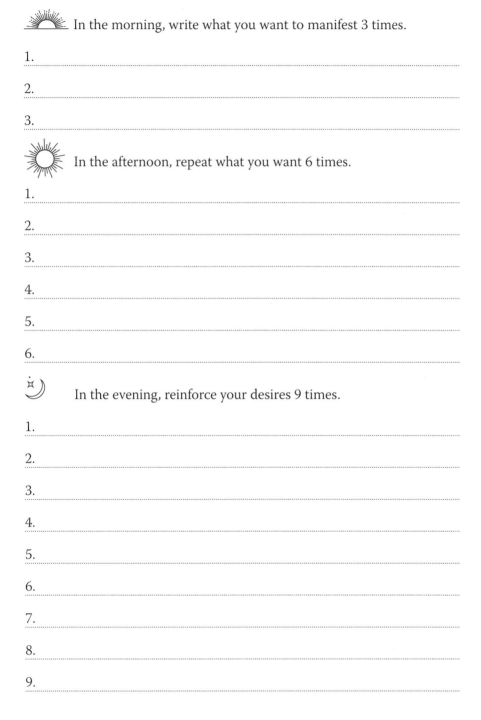 In the morning, write what you want to manifest 3 times.

1. ....

2. ....

3. ....

In the afternoon, repeat what you want 6 times.

1. ....

2. ....

3. ....

4. ....

5. ....

6. ....

In the evening, reinforce your desires 9 times.

1. ....

2. ....

3. ....

4. ....

5. ....

6. ....

7. ....

8. ....

9. ....

Week 13

Create Something New

*"Every thing and institution we see around us,
created by human agency, had first to exist
as a thought in some human mind."*

**—F. H. Burgess, in his introduction to Charles
F. Haanel's *The Master Key System***

As mentioned in Week 6, having a creative imagination can contribute greatly to your success. Creativity helps your mind make connections between things that previously seemed unconnected. This, in turn, helps you to come up with unique ideas and become a better problem-solver. And the even better news is that creativity is something you can work on and improve.

Exercise: Look around you and pick any two objects. Spend a few minutes brainstorming ways to combine them into new products. Be as silly as you like. And feel free to sketch your new creations. Expand your creativity to make you better able to handle issues that arise while working toward your manifestation goals.

Object 1:

....

Object 2:

....

New products:

....

....

....

369 Manifestations

In the morning, write what you want to manifest 3 times.

1.

2.

3.

In the afternoon, repeat what you want 6 times.

1.

2.

3.

4.

5.

6.

In the evening, reinforce your desires 9 times.

1.

2.

3.

4.

5.

6.

7.

8.

9.

Week 14

Count Your Blessings

*"When I started counting my blessings,
my whole life turned around."*

—Willie Nelson

It is time to reflect on things for which you are grateful once again. Gratitude journaling is known to provide both mental and physical health benefits. It's also easy to do. Just think about anything that's good in your life, big or small, and write down a statement of gratitude for it.

Think about positive things that have happened recently, loved ones you feel lucky to have in your life, or accomplishments you have made. Do you get to partake in hobbies or pastimes you enjoy? Do you like your job or coworkers? Are you grateful for that morning cup of coffee that gets you through the day? Anything that meets your needs or brings you pleasure or happiness counts!

Exercise: Reflect on and jot down three or more things for which you are grateful. If you can think of more than three, that's great! Write away! Feel free to include any that will make it easier to reach this week's manifestation goals.

I'm grateful for

....

....

....

....

I'm grateful for

....

....

....

....

I'm grateful for

....

....

....

....

....

....

....

....

369 Manifestations

In the morning, write what you want to manifest 3 times.

1.

2.

3.

In the afternoon, repeat what you want 6 times.

1.

2.

3.

4.

5.

6.

In the evening, reinforce your desires 9 times.

1.

2.

3.

4.

5.

6.

7.

8.

9.

Week 15

Meditate Mindfully

"Tension is who you think you should be. Relaxation is who you are."

—Chinese proverb

Mindfulness meditation seeks to bring your focus to the present rather than letting it dwell in the past or on future worries. Guided meditations (which can be found on CD, online, via streaming services, or through phone apps) are especially helpful if you are new to the practice. You might even be able to find relevant guided meditations by searching for things like "manifestation meditation" or "Law of Attraction meditation." The following is a simple body-scan mindfulness meditation session that incorporates head-to-toe relaxation, with a bonus visualization.

Exercise: Follow these simple steps:

1. Lie on your back on a comfortable surface or sit upright in a comfortable position.

2. Close your eyes and spend a minute or so focusing on your breathing. Notice how it feels when you breathe in and out. If thoughts invade, let them come, allow them to pass without self-judgment, and return your focus to your breathing.

3. Spend a few minutes relaxing each part of your body in turn, starting at the top of your head and moving slowly all the way to your toes, or vice versa. Notice how each area feels, try to release any tension you encounter there, and move on to the next area.

4. Once you have relaxed your body, place yourself into a pleasant daydream where you have fulfilled the goals from this week's chosen manifestation statement. Fill it with the sights, sounds, and other sensations of your dream life. Stay in this reverie for a few minutes.

5. Open your eyes.

6. Write down how you feel and try to retain the positive feelings when repeating your desired manifestations this week.

369 Manifestations

In the morning, write what you want to manifest 3 times.

1. ....

2. ....

3. ....

In the afternoon, repeat what you want 6 times.

1. ....

2. ....

3. ....

4. ....

5. ....

6. ....

In the evening, reinforce your desires 9 times.

1. ....

2. ....

3. ....

4. ....

5. ....

6. ....

7. ....

8. ....

9. ....

Week 16

Take Positive Baby Steps

"You miss 100 percent of the shots you don't take."
**—Wayne Gretzky, former professional ice
hockey player and head coach**

The path to your goals can seem long and difficult if you think about everything that is required to get there all at once. It is better to break down large projects into multiple small tasks that you can address one at a time. You also need to find workarounds for any obstacles standing in your way. For example, if you feel like you don't have time to work on your passion, one remedy might be to spend fifteen minutes of your lunch break working on one of the smaller steps. If your home is full of distractions, maybe put in a few minutes in your car in the work parking lot or your driveway. Baby-step your way closer to your desires.

Exercise: Write down three or more possible actions that relate to your chosen manifestation. If there is anything standing in the way of each action, write the obstacle, then brainstorm solutions. Pick one action, and its obstacles, to tackle in the coming week.

Action

....

....

Obstacle

....

....

Solutions

....

....

Action

....

....

Obstacle

....

....

Solutions

....

....

Action

....

....

Obstacle

....

....

Solutions

....

....

....

369 Manifestations

In the morning, write what you want to manifest 3 times.

1. ....

2. ....

3. ....

In the afternoon, repeat what you want 6 times.

1. ....

2. ....

3. ....

4. ....

5. ....

6. ....

In the evening, reinforce your desires 9 times.

1. ....

2. ....

3. ....

4. ....

5. ....

6. ....

7. ....

8. ....

9. ....

Week 17

Give Back

"Anything you can imagine, you can create."
—Oprah Winfrey

Receiving what you want isn't the only good thing in life. In fact, giving things, money, and help to others has been shown in studies to provide health benefits to the giver, including increased happiness, reduced stress, and decreased risk of death (Suttie and Marsh 2010). Being generous also strengthens social connections, which are important to overall well-being. This week, focus on giving as much as on manifesting your desires. You'll be better off for it.

Exercise: Give something to someone or to an entity. It can be money to a charity, time to a cause, a gift to a loved one, emotional support to a friend, or help to a neighbor. There are lots of ways to give back. Afterward, make a note of how it made you feel. Reflect on how achieving this week's manifestation goal could allow you to make the world a better place.

369 Manifestations

In the morning, write what you want to manifest 3 times.

1. ....

2. ....

3. ....

In the afternoon, repeat what you want 6 times.

1. ....

2. ....

3. ....

4. ....

5. ....

6. ....

In the evening, reinforce your desires 9 times.

1. ....

2. ....

3. ....

4. ....

5. ....

6. ....

7. ....

8. ....

9. ....

Week 18

Get Moving, and Get Creative

"Physical fitness is the first requisite of happiness."

—Joseph Pilates

It's time for physical exercise once again! This doubles as a creativity exercise because physical activity increases creativity and innovation. Whether it's because activity gets more oxygen to your brain or something else, we don't know the exact mechanism. We do know people do better on creative tasks during and after physical exercise. Many successful people swear by walking for spurring their minds to come up with new ideas. When you are working on a problem or project that requires creative thinking, try pondering it while walking. Or, pick another activity that gets your body (and your brain) moving.

Exercise: Think about a problem or something you'd like to brainstorm, especially something related to this week's manifestation statement. Jot it down, and get moving! Walk, dance, stretch, wave your arms about—it's your choice. Try to come up with ideas during and after your physical exercise that could help you manifest your desires. Write what you come up with below.

Think about...

_____

_____

_____

_____

_____

_____

_____

369 Manifestations

In the morning, write what you want to manifest 3 times.

1. ....

2. ....

3. ....

In the afternoon, repeat what you want 6 times.

1. ....

2. ....

3. ....

4. ....

5. ....

6. ....

In the evening, reinforce your desires 9 times.

1. ....

2. ....

3. ....

4. ....

5. ....

6. ....

7. ....

8. ....

9. ....

Week 19

Affirm Your Worth

"Believe in yourself. You are braver than you think, more talented than you know, and capable of more than you imagine."

—Roy T. Bennett, positivity author

It's time once again for positive affirmations! As mentioned, they can help bolster your self-esteem, reduce stress, and make you more resilient when things go wrong. If you are having negative thoughts about your ability to reach your manifestation goals, write positive affirmations that directly refute them.

Exercise: Think about this week's manifestation goals. Do any feelings of doubt or uncertainty surface? Use these feelings to craft positive affirmations that negate them. For instance, if you doubt your skills in relation to your goals, you might refute that doubt with "I am a resourceful and intelligent human being who can learn new skills." You can make your affirmations more detailed, personal, and relevant to your current goals. Say them aloud several times. Or, write them again, if you prefer. Feel free to do this anytime your inner critic is making you doubt your ability to manifest your chosen desires.

369 Manifestations

In the morning, write what you want to manifest 3 times.

1.

2.

3.

In the afternoon, repeat what you want 6 times.

1.

2.

3.

4.

5.

6.

In the evening, reinforce your desires 9 times.

1.

2.

3.

4.

5.

6.

7.

8.

9.

Week 20

Take Time for Yourself

"Love yourself first, and everything else falls in line. You really have to love yourself to get anything done in this world."

—Lucille Ball

Self-care is important. And one oft-overlooked form of self-care is taking time for yourself. Spend a little quality time alone, away from the distractions of daily life. Schedule it like an appointment. If you have a door, shut it. If you can't resist electronic devices, turn off your phone, computer, or television for the duration. If you can't get alone time at home or at the office, go to a park or library. And you don't have to totally isolate for quality me time. You can even sit alone in a coffee shop or restaurant to think or read. This solitude can help you relax, clear your head, think more deeply about things, and learn more about yourself and what you want out of life.

Exercise: Make an appointment and spend some quality time with yourself. You can sit and think, or do a solitary activity you enjoy. For instance, you might treat yourself to a spa treatment, practice a solo hobby, or make a cup of tea and curl up in a comfy chair with a good book. Afterward, write down how the solitude made you feel and what thoughts came to mind. And take advantage of this momentum to craft this week's manifestation statement.

369 Manifestations

In the morning, write what you want to manifest 3 times.

1. ....

2. ....

3. ....

In the afternoon, repeat what you want 6 times.

1. ....

2. ....

3. ....

4. ....

5. ....

6. ....

In the evening, reinforce your desires 9 times.

1. ....

2. ....

3. ....

4. ....

5. ....

6. ....

7. ....

8. ....

9. ....

Week 21

Draw Something New

"If you fall in love with the imagination, you understand that it is a free spirit. It will go anywhere, and it can do anything."

—Alice Walker

As you have read in previous sections, it is important to stimulate your imagination and creativity on a regular basis. This week we'll focus on drawing once again, this time with prompts. And don't worry about or harshly critique your results. You don't have to be a skilled artist to let your imagination flow out onto the paper. Just doing it will stir your imagination.

Exercise: Look at the following images. Do they bring anything to mind? Use the shapes below to draw new objects that incorporate them. You can make them into separate drawings or connect them however you'd like. Afterward, use your newly stimulated creativity to craft this week's manifestation statement.

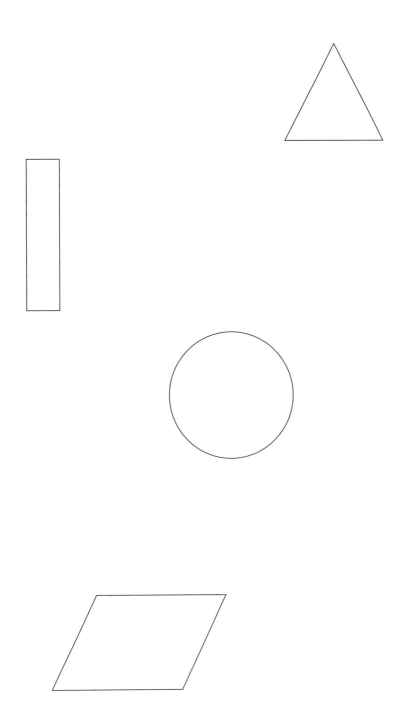

369 Manifestations

In the morning, write what you want to manifest 3 times.

1. ....

2. ....

3. ....

In the afternoon, repeat what you want 6 times.

1. ....

2. ....

3. ....

4. ....

5. ....

6. ....

In the evening, reinforce your desires 9 times.

1. ....

2. ....

3. ....

4. ....

5. ....

6. ....

7. ....

8. ....

9. ....

Week 22

Meditate with Loving-Kindness

"Meditation is not about stopping thoughts, but recognizing that we are more than our thoughts and our feelings."

—Arianna Huffington

There are many types of mindfulness meditation. One is the Metta meditation, from the Buddhist term meaning "loving-kindness." Loving-kindness meditation has been shown to increase motivation, empathy, and positive emotions (like happiness and love), and to decrease self-destructive thoughts and even symptoms of physical pain. All it requires is a quiet, comfortable spot where you can rest for a few minutes and chant loving phrases to yourself, like "May I be safe," "May I be at peace," "May I be strong," "May I be well," or "May I achieve my desires."

Feel free to adopt these or make up your own. And when you say the words, think about what they mean. You really want to feel the kindness behind them. You may also direct phrases toward others (people you like, people you don't like, or the entire world) by changing "I" to "you" or "all" in your chosen phrases.

Exercise: Do the following:

1. Before meditating, write down how you feel.

2. Find a quiet spot and sit or lie in a comfortable position.

3. Set a timer for two minutes or more.

4. Softly say the kind and loving phrases of your choice to yourself until the timer runs out. Feel free to switch to directing the phrases to others before your time is up.

5. Repeat daily for continued results.

6. Write down how you feel after the meditation, and, while you still have your writing utensil out, use this opportunity to write down this week's manifestation statement.

Before:

....

....

....

....

After:

....

....

....

....

369 Manifestations

In the morning, write what you want to manifest 3 times.

1. ....

2. ....

3. ....

In the afternoon, repeat what you want 6 times.

1. ....

2. ....

3. ....

4. ....

5. ....

6. ....

In the evening, reinforce your desires 9 times.

1. ....

2. ....

3. ....

4. ....

5. ....

6. ....

7. ....

8. ....

9. ....

Reflect on What Makes You Happy

*"Reflect upon your present blessings—of which
every man has many—not on your past
misfortunes, of which all men have some."*

—Charles Dickens

It's gratitude time again! Jot down good things that have happened to you lately, or the little things in life that make you happy.

Do you have loved ones who bring you joy? Do you get to enjoy the pleasures of a good book (or TV show, movie, or game) every now and then? Have you caught any lucky breaks? Any new accomplishments? All are welcome on your gratitude list.

Exercise: Reflect on and list off three or more things for which you are grateful. If you can think of more than three, wonderful! Write as many as you'd like, and hold on to the good feeling gratitude gives you while you write out your manifestation statement this week.

I'm grateful for

....

....

....

....

I'm grateful for

....

....

....

....

I'm grateful for

....

....

....

....

....

....

....

....

369 Manifestations

In the morning, write what you want to manifest 3 times.

1. ....

2. ....

3. ....

In the afternoon, repeat what you want 6 times.

1. ....

2. ....

3. ....

4. ....

5. ....

6. ....

In the evening, reinforce your desires 9 times.

1. ....

2. ....

3. ....

4. ....

5. ....

6. ....

7. ....

8. ....

9. ....

Week 24

Visualize Your Dream Job

"Trust yourself. Create the kind of self that you will be happy to live with all your life. Make the most of yourself by fanning the tiny, inner sparks of possibility into flames of achievement."

—Golda Meir, former prime minister of Israel

Visualize your dream job in as much detail as possible and involving all your senses. What does your desired work environment include? What sights, sounds, textures, scents, and tastes are there? Imagine yourself doing your desired tasks. Use this technique to keep your inner eye on the prize.

Exercise: Get into a comfortable position, close your eyes, and envision yourself doing what you want to be doing in your dream job (whether it's writing an epic novel or helping others through a nonprofit organization). Imagine the sights, sounds, aromas, tastes, and textures as you go about your work day. Afterward, write down the details you remember, note how you felt during the visualization, and use this momentum to create your manifestation statement for the week.

369 Manifestations

In the morning, write what you want to manifest 3 times.

1. _____

2. _____

3. _____

In the afternoon, repeat what you want 6 times.

1. _____

2. _____

3. _____

4. _____

5. _____

6. _____

In the evening, reinforce your desires 9 times.

1. _____

2. _____

3. _____

4. _____

5. _____

6. _____

7. _____

8. _____

9. _____

Week 25

Question Negative Self-Talk

"If you are insecure, guess what? The rest of the world is, too. Do not overestimate the competition and underestimate yourself. You are better than you think."

—Timothy Ferriss, from his book *The 4-Hour Workweek*

All of us are plagued by doubts and negative self-talk every now and then. Many of our fears and doubts are unfounded. Don't let the thoughts themselves defeat you. When a negative idea is causing you stress or deflating your self-esteem, don't give in or give up. Interrogate these intrusive thoughts to help yourself see them in a different light.

Exercise: Write down a negative self-talk that is fueling your self-doubt. Then answer three or more of the following questions about it.

Thought: ....

1. What evidence backs up this thought? What evidence refutes it?

....

....

2. What assumptions am I making?

....

....

3. Are there other possible points of view? If so, what are they?

....

....

4. Is this thought based on feelings or facts?

....

....

5. Is the thought black and white, or does it represent the complexities of reality?

....

....

6. What led you to think this thought? Have you always thought it?

....

....

7. If the thought were true, what would the consequences be?

....

....

After questioning your thought, do you see things differently? Is the thought now less scary? Try to write out one or more positive spins on the thought. And feel free to use that positive spin to inspire your weekly manifestation statement.

1. Positive Spin

2. Positive Spin

3. Positive Spin

4. Positive Spin

5. Positive Spin

6. Positive Spin

7. Positive Spin

369 Manifestations

In the morning, write what you want to manifest 3 times.

1.
2.
3.

In the afternoon, repeat what you want 6 times.

1.
2.
3.
4.
5.
6.

In the evening, reinforce your desires 9 times.

1.
2.
3.
4.
5.
6.
7.
8.
9.

Week 26

Rediscover What You Want

"Ask for what you want and be prepared to get it."

—Maya Angelou

You're halfway through the journal! Time to reassess your goals and see if they still fit. Have you changed? Have circumstances changed? Have you already reached a goal, and do you need to pick a new one? Whatever the case, it's never a bad idea to reassess your life and aspirations and figure out what you want to work toward.

If you have any trouble coming up with your new wants, you can repeat the exercise from Week 1. Think of things you *don't* like that are holding you back and brainstorm goals that would counteract them.

Exercise: List several things that you don't like or that aren't working for you on the left. Then, to the right of each, write something to strive for that would help alleviate that. Keep these refactored goals in mind for future manifestation and visualization exercises.

Dislikes   **Remedies**

....

....

....

....

....

....

....

....

....

369 Manifestations

In the morning, write what you want to manifest 3 times.

1. ....

2. ....

3. ....

In the afternoon, repeat what you want 6 times.

1. ....

2. ....

3. ....

4. ....

5. ....

6. ....

In the evening, reinforce your desires 9 times.

1. ....

2. ....

3. ....

4. ....

5. ....

6. ....

7. ....

8. ....

9. ....

Reward Small Milestones

"The way to develop self-confidence is to do the thing you fear and get a record of successful experiences behind you."

—William Jennings Bryan, former US secretary of state

One way to achieve your goals is to take small—even tiny—steps that get you closer to them. A bunch of small steps eventually add up to a larger accomplishment. But it also helps to provide yourself with incentive. One way is to reward yourself when you reach a mini milestone. Buy yourself a gift or enjoy a favorite leisure activity (such as TV or video games) as a reward for accomplishing a step or working on your goal for a set amount of time. Take a step, then treat yourself.

Exercise: Make a bargain with yourself this week to treat yourself for every step taken or time period spent working toward your desires. Below, write down that bargain. Afterward, come up with a manifestation statement inspired by your planned step.

When I
....

I will reward myself with
....

....

....

369 Manifestations

In the morning, write what you want to manifest 3 times.

1.

2.

3.

In the afternoon, repeat what you want 6 times.

1.

2.

3.

4.

5.

6.

In the evening, reinforce your desires 9 times.

1.

2.

3.

4.

5.

6.

7.

8.

9.

Week 28

Exude Self-Confidence

"To be yourself in a world that is constantly trying to make you something else is the greatest accomplishment."

—Ralph Waldo Emerson

Drive away negative self-talk by talking yourself up—to yourself! A positive, self-confident attitude is one key to manifesting your desires. You are a capable person worthy of achieving your goals.

Feel good about yourself and have a positive outlook on life, and you can handle anything that comes your way.

Exercise: Think up and jot down one to several positive affirmations, such as "I have a lot of love in my life," "I am capable of achieving my dreams," or "I have a wealth of knowledge and skills." You can make them more detailed, personal, and relevant to your current manifestation goals. Say your affirmation(s) aloud several times, think them to yourself on repeat, or write them a few times if you prefer. Feel free to do this anytime your inner critic is interfering with your current aspirations.

369 Manifestations

In the morning, write what you want to manifest 3 times.

1.

2.

3.

In the afternoon, repeat what you want 6 times.

1.

2.

3.

4.

5.

6.

In the evening, reinforce your desires 9 times.

1.

2.

3.

4.

5.

6.

7.

8.

9.

Week 29

15 Minutes of Movement

*"It is health that is the real wealth, and
not pieces of gold and silver."*

—Mahatma Gandhi

Use the mental benefits of exercise to keep you on your path to manifesting your desires. Think of the physical benefits as a bonus and get that oxygen-rich blood pumping to stimulate your mind.

Exercise: Do fifteen minutes of the physical activity of your choice: martial arts, badminton with a friend, disco dancing, a simple walk around the block—whatever suits your mood and your current ability. Also try to think about your current goals or projects and, afterward, write any ideas that jogged loose during the activity.

Think about...

....

....

....

....

....

369 Manifestations

In the morning, write what you want to manifest 3 times.

1.

2.

3.

In the afternoon, repeat what you want 6 times.

1.

2.

3.

4.

5.

6.

In the evening, reinforce your desires 9 times.

1.

2.

3.

4.

5.

6.

7.

8.

9.

Week 30

Feed Your Mind

"What is now proved was once only imagined."
—William Blake

One way to foster your creativity is to feed your mind new information. You can study new topics via online or in-person classes, books, audiobooks, documentaries, and the like. The more things you learn and think about, the more new connections your mind can make, and the more you can imagine new things to bring into reality.

Exercise: Pick a topic you know little to nothing about. Do a Google search and read articles, peruse websites, or watch videos about it until you learn something new. Did the topic elicit mental images? Did you connect any of this new information with your existing knowledge, life, or goals? Write a paragraph (fact or fiction) about anything the new topic brought to mind. Feel free to doodle images, too. Afterward, use this creative momentum to write a new manifestation statement.

369 Manifestations

In the morning, write what you want to manifest 3 times.

1. ....

2. ....

3. ....

In the afternoon, repeat what you want 6 times.

1. ....

2. ....

3. ....

4. ....

5. ....

6. ....

In the evening, reinforce your desires 9 times.

1. ....

2. ....

3. ....

4. ....

5. ....

6. ....

7. ....

8. ....

9. ....

Week 31

Sitting Meditation

*"Remain calm in every situation,
because peace equals power."*

—Joyce Meyer, author and speaker

This week's mindfulness exercise is sitting meditation. Reap the mental and physical benefits of mindfulness meditation from the comfort of your favorite chair or floor pillow! As ever, the goal is to focus your attention on something (in the case of this exercise, your breathing, but you can also focus on other sensations, including sounds, thoughts, or emotions). When your mind wanders (as it is bound to do), note the thought without self-judgment and return your attention to your chosen area of focus. Feel free to find a guided sitting meditation, or to follow the steps below.

Exercise: Do the following:

1. Jot down how you feel before this exercise.

2. Find a comfortable sitting position. It can be in a chair or on the floor on a mat or pillow, or even a meditation stool if you have one.

3. Breathe naturally. Focus on your breath and notice the sensations it causes. Where do you feel it the most? The nose? The chest? The diaphragm? Try to keep your focus on the feeling of your breath in that area.

4. When your mind wanders, acknowledge the thoughts and dismiss them without self-criticism.

5. Continue for five to ten minutes.

6. Afterward, jot down how you feel again after this exercise. Then write out your manifestation statement for the week.

Before

....

....

....

....

After:

....

....

....

....

Manifestation statement:

....

....

....

....

369 Manifestations

In the morning, write what you want to manifest 3 times.

1. ....

2. ....

3. ....

In the afternoon, repeat what you want 6 times.

1. ....

2. ....

3. ....

4. ....

5. ....

6. ....

In the evening, reinforce your desires 9 times.

1. ....

2. ....

3. ....

4. ....

5. ....

6. ....

7. ....

8. ....

9. ....

Week 32

Anticipate Good Things

*"A thankful heart is not only the greatest virtue,
but the parent of all the other virtues."*

—Cicero

What are you grateful for today? As you know from previous sections, regularly expressing gratitude brings a number of benefits. Think about good things and good people in your life, or good experiences or events that have happened in the past.

Now, consider the things you regularly look forward to, like spending time with loved ones or enjoying a good meal. Are good things happening at work or at home? Have you learned anything new? Have you discovered a tasty new beverage? Nothing is too big or too small for gratitude.

Exercise: Think about and write down three or more things you look forward to. If you come up with more than three, great! Write to your heart's content. Afterward, while in the glow of gratitude, use your already-busy pen to write out your manifestation statement.

I'm grateful for

....

....

....

....

....

I'm grateful for

....

....

....

....

....

I'm grateful for

....

....

....

....

....

....

....

....

369 Manifestations

In the morning, write what you want to manifest 3 times.

1. ....

2. ....

3. ....

In the afternoon, repeat what you want 6 times.

1. ....

2. ....

3. ....

4. ....

5. ....

6. ....

In the evening, reinforce your desires 9 times.

1. ....

2. ....

3. ....

4. ....

5. ....

6. ....

7. ....

8. ....

9. ....

Week 33

See Success in Your Mind's Eye

"You are more productive by doing fifteen minutes of visualization than from sixteen hours of hard labor."

—Abraham Hicks

Use visualization to keep your conscious and unconscious mind pointed toward your manifestation goals. And to get a taste of success in your mind's eye.

Exercise: What does success look and feel like to you? While in a comfortable position, close your eyes and envision yourself having achieved the sights, sounds, aromas, tastes, and textures of a fulfilled heart. Afterward, write down what you remember, and note how the dream vision made you feel. Then fill out your manifestation statement for the week.

....

....

....

....

....

369 Manifestations

In the morning, write what you want to manifest 3 times.

1.

2.

3.

In the afternoon, repeat what you want 6 times.

1.

2.

3.

4.

5.

6.

In the evening, reinforce your desires 9 times.

1.

2.

3.

4.

5.

6.

7.

8.

9.

Week 34

Spread Generosity

"There is no exercise better for the heart than reaching down and lifting people up."

—John Holmes, author and veteran

Generosity has been linked to mental and physical health benefits, feelings of happiness, and stronger bonds with others. One possible reason is that it induces release of the hormone oxytocin, which causes feelings of euphoria and connection to other people.

Giving is also contagious. One study found that generosity inspires generosity in others and can spread from person to person in a network (Suttie and Marsh 2010). Give and make your community a better place. And it may even spread back to you eventually.

Exercise: Give something of yourself: money, time, moral support, or help. Whatever you can afford. After your act of giving, write down how it made you feel. Feel free to repeat this exercise and spread the contagion of generosity. Think about how you can help others once you achieve your dreams and keep this spirit of giving in mind while crafting your manifestation statement this week.

369 Manifestations

In the morning, write what you want to manifest 3 times.

1. ....
2. ....
3. ....

In the afternoon, repeat what you want 6 times.

1. ....
2. ....
3. ....
4. ....
5. ....
6. ....

In the evening, reinforce your desires 9 times.

1. ....
2. ....
3. ....
4. ....
5. ....
6. ....
7. ....
8. ....
9. ....

Week 35

Show Yourself Kindness

"Talk to yourself like you would to someone you love."
—Brené Brown

Showing yourself kindness has been shown to decrease anxiety and increase resilience. If you've been feeling down or have negative thoughts about any perceived faults or missteps in life, know that you are human, and we all do these things and feel this way sometimes. Everything that happens, good or bad, can be used as a life lesson. Go easy on yourself and practice self-care whenever you need it. To err is human. To forgive yourself divine.

Exercise: Write yourself a note as if it were from a loved one, forgiving any faults and contradicting any harsh criticisms you have of yourself. Make it loving and compassionate. Read your note back to yourself and try to take it to heart. Then, write out this week's manifestation statement while basking in the warm glow of self-compassion.

369 Manifestations

In the morning, write what you want to manifest 3 times.

1. ....

2. ....

3. ....

In the afternoon, repeat what you want 6 times.

1. ....

2. ....

3. ....

4. ....

5. ....

6. ....

In the evening, reinforce your desires 9 times.

1. ....

2. ....

3. ....

4. ....

5. ....

6. ....

7. ....

8. ....

9. ....

Week 36

Practice Accountability

"If you hear a voice within you say 'you cannot paint,'
then by all means paint, and that voice will be silenced."

—Vincent Van Gogh

One thing that helps people perform rather than procrastinate is accountability. If you tell someone you plan to do something, you are more likely to do it. You can tell an intention to a friend or relative (someone who has been supportive in the past), announce it to the world on social media, or find a partner willing to hold you accountable in exchange for doing the same for them. You can even make a contract with them, with a small penalty for any agreed-upon tasks you fail to do. For instance, each might cost you a $5 donation to charity, or a chore you must do for the other person. There are even accountability apps you can try. Find the accountability method that resonates with you.

Exercise: Write down one or more micro-goals you want to achieve this week. Then, pick an accountability method you want to try and do it. Write down the accountability method. And feel free to try others, too. Different things work for different people.

Task(s)

....

....

....

....

....

Accountability Method(s)

....

....

....

....

....

....

....

....

....

....

369 Manifestations

In the morning, write what you want to manifest 3 times.

1.

2.

3.

In the afternoon, repeat what you want 6 times.

1.

2.

3.

4.

5.

6.

In the evening, reinforce your desires 9 times.

1.

2.

3.

4.

5.

6.

7.

8.

9.

Week 37

Believe in Yourself

"Optimism is the faith that leads to achievement.
Nothing can be done without hope and confidence."
—Helen Keller

It's time to give yourself a mental boost with positive affirmations. They have been shown to improve self-esteem, which is an important factor in achieving your goals. Believing you can do things is one of the first steps to doing them.

Relate your present-tense, positive statements to your current goals or your general worthiness. Tell yourself how awesome you are!

Exercise: Come up with one to several positive affirmations, such as "I am the best," "I have the world on a string," or "I am a kind and loving person." They can be more detailed, personal, and relevant to your current goals if you like. Repeat them several times aloud, on paper, or in your head. Feel free to break out this exercise anytime self-doubt rears its head. Use this newly fueled self-confidence to write your weekly manifestation statement.

I am…

I have…

369 Manifestations

In the morning, write what you want to manifest 3 times.

1. ....

2. ....

3. ....

In the afternoon, repeat what you want 6 times.

1. ....

2. ....

3. ....

4. ....

5. ....

6. ....

In the evening, reinforce your desires 9 times.

1. ....

2. ....

3. ....

4. ....

5. ....

6. ....

7. ....

8. ....

9. ....

Week 38

15 Minutes of Movement

"Without leaps of imagination, or dreaming, we lose the excitement of possibilities. Dreaming, after all, is a form of planning."
—Gloria Steinem

Boost your mood and spur your mind to generate new ideas with a bit of action.

Exercise: Do a physical activity of your choice, such as tennis with a friend, marching in place, calisthenics, salsa dancing, or that tried-and-true classic: walking. Try to move for about fifteen minutes and think about your desires during the activity. Afterward, brainstorm tasks you can do related to your desired manifestation, or any other ideas that arise.

Brainstorm

369 Manifestations

In the morning, write what you want to manifest 3 times.

1.

2.

3.

In the afternoon, repeat what you want 6 times.

1.

2.

3.

4.

5.

6.

In the evening, reinforce your desires 9 times.

1.

2.

3.

4.

5.

6.

7.

8.

9.

Week 39

Flex Your Creative Muscles

*"Imagination is more important that knowledge.
Knowledge is limited. Imagination encircles the world."*

—Albert Einstein

It's time for more creative play! As you well know by now, creativity is a gift that keeps giving—and an ability that you can foster and grow. Being able to imagine new products, ideas, or states of being and doing is key to innovation. Whatever you want to do or create, you need to be able to conceptualize first, so it's important to flex the creative muscles regularly.

Exercise: Starting with the first circle, sketch whatever new item you can think of. Continue with each of the circles below until they are all filled. Afterward, use your recently exercised imagination to write this week's manifestation statement.

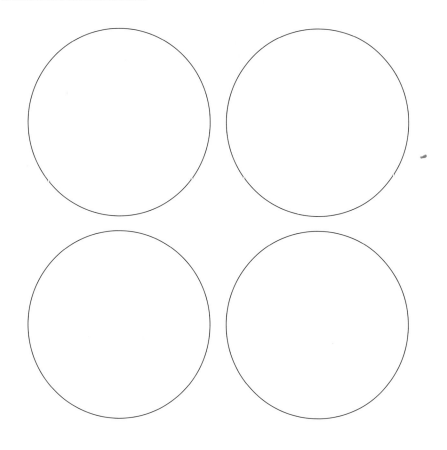

Manifestation Statement

....

....

....

....

....

369 Manifestations

 In the morning, write what you want to manifest 3 times.

1.

2.

3.

In the afternoon, repeat what you want 6 times.

1.

2.

3.

4.

5.

6.

In the evening, reinforce your desires 9 times.

1.

2.

3.

4.

5.

6.

7.

8.

9.

Visualize Self-Care

"Everything you can imagine is real."

—Pablo Picasso

You don't always have to visualize yourself in relation to your achievements. You can also use visualization as a relaxation technique. Time for a little self-care in the form of a relaxing vision. Go to your happy place and dwell there for a while in your mind. You deserve a mental vacation.

Exercise: Follow these simple steps:

1. Get into a comfortable position.

2. Close your eyes.

3. Imagine a peaceful place you enjoy (or would enjoy) going. It can be real or made up—a cabin, a beach, a clearing in the woods, or whatever setting brings you peace.

4. Imagine the setting in detail with all your senses. What do you see, feel, hear, smell, and taste? If any thoughts interfere, acknowledge them, let them pass, and resume visualizing your chosen surroundings.

5. Stay in this reverie for a few minutes.

6. Open your eyes and resume your day.

7. Write how you feel and use the momentum to write your weekly manifestation statement.

....

....

....

....

....

....

....

....

369 Manifestations

In the morning, write what you want to manifest 3 times.

1. ....

2. ....

3. ....

In the afternoon, repeat what you want 6 times.

1. ....

2. ....

3. ....

4. ....

5. ....

6. ....

In the evening, reinforce your desires 9 times.

1. ....

2. ....

3. ....

4. ....

5. ....

6. ....

7. ....

8. ....

9. ....

Week 41

Express Your Gratitude

"This is a wonderful day. I have never seen this one before."

—Maya Angelou

It's time once again to express your gratitude! As you now well know, regularly expressing gratefulness has been linked to a host of mental, physical, and interpersonal benefits.

Think about any good things that have come into your life. Have you made any accomplishments, minor or major? Are you feeling good about any aspect of yourself? Do you have human or furry companions who enhance your enjoyment of life? Do you get to partake in your favorite foods every now and again? Show gratitude for anything that brings you any amount of comfort or joy.

Exercise: Ponder and jot down three or more things for which you are grateful. If you have more than three, fantastic! The limit does not exist! Carry the good feelings your gratitude brings to you into writing this week's manifestation statement.

I'm grateful for

....

....

....

....

....

I'm grateful for

....

....

....

....

....

I'm grateful for

....

....

....

....

....

....

....

....

....

369 Manifestations

In the morning, write what you want to manifest 3 times.

1. ....

2. ....

3. ....

In the afternoon, repeat what you want 6 times.

1. ....

2. ....

3. ....

4. ....

5. ....

6. ....

In the evening, reinforce your desires 9 times.

1. ....

2. ....

3. ....

4. ....

5. ....

6. ....

7. ....

8. ....

9. ....

Week 42

Meditate Mindfully While Walking

"Quiet the mind, and the soul will speak."

—Ma Jaya Sati Bhagavati, spiritual teacher, activist, and author

Another type of mindfulness meditation is walking meditation. One of the goals of mindfulness is to make you aware of things you might not normally pay attention to, like things going on with your body and mind as you exist in your surroundings. In the case of walking meditation, the aim is to focus on the act of walking while pacing slowly back and forth for a few minutes—indoors or outdoors—and preferably away from other people. You can do it in your house, your yard, or your favorite walking path. Reap the benefits of mindfulness meditation with bonus physical activity.

Exercise: Do the following (or if you prefer, search for and use a guided walking meditation):

1. Write how you feel before starting the walking meditation.

2. Find a spot where you can walk at least ten paces in a straight line.

3. Walk slowly and rhythmically (but naturally) while paying attention to the feelings of several distinct parts of the motion (your leg and foot lifting off the ground, your foot and body moving forward, the placing of your

heel on the ground, your weight shifting onto that foot as you lift the other foot, and so on). As with any meditation, if thoughts intrude, let them come, dismiss them, and turn your focus back to the meditation.

4. When you run out of space, stop, take a few breaths and focus on the sensations of breathing.

5. Turn and walk back the way you came at the same pace and focusing on the same things.

6. Repeat this over and over for around ten minutes.

7. Write how you feel after the walking meditation, then use your newfound focus to write this week's manifestation statement.

Before

....

....

....

....

....

After

....

....

....

....

....

....

369 Manifestations

In the morning, write what you want to manifest 3 times.

1. ....

2. ....

3. ....

In the afternoon, repeat what you want 6 times.

1. ....

2. ....

3. ....

4. ....

5. ....

6. ....

In the evening, reinforce your desires 9 times.

1. ....

2. ....

3. ....

4. ....

5. ....

6. ....

7. ....

8. ....

9. ....

Week 43

Visualize Your Desired Future

"Confidence is a habit that can be developed by acting as if you already had the confidence you desire to have."

—Brian Tracy, motivational speaker

It's time once again to pretend you have already manifested your desires. Take your future life for a test-drive by visualizing it. Include sights, sounds, textures, scents, and tastes that would be present in your desired future. Use visualization to keep your conscious and unconscious mind moving toward your manifestation goals. And spend a few minutes reveling in the pleasant sensations of living your dreams.

Exercise: Get into a comfortable position, close your eyes, and envision yourself having achieved your desires. Envision aspects of the scene that involve all your senses. Afterward, write down what you remember and how the visualization session made you feel. Use this vision to construct this week's manifestation statement.

369 Manifestations

In the morning, write what you want to manifest 3 times.

1. ....

2. ....

3. ....

In the afternoon, repeat what you want 6 times.

1. ....

2. ....

3. ....

4. ....

5. ....

6. ....

In the evening, reinforce your desires 9 times.

1. ....

2. ....

3. ....

4. ....

5. ....

6. ....

7. ....

8. ....

9. ....

Week 44

Practice Positive Self-Talk

"To love oneself is the beginning of a lifelong romance."
—Oscar Wilde

Most of us think negative thoughts about ourselves on the regular. When you make a mistake, you might say to yourself, "I'm stupid," and when you have a career setback, you might think, "I'm a failure." Your inner critic is a harsh one and repeating and internalizing these negative messages can fuel self-doubt and stress. When you catch yourself spouting negative self-talk, try to spin it around. For instance, if you make a mistake at work, rather than berating yourself, note that the fact that you care shows that you are a conscientious worker. And remember that you are human. We all make mistakes. It's how we deal with them that matters most. So be kind to yourself.

Exercise: Think of negative messages you have thought or told to yourself in the past. Write them down. Then spin them into positive statements about yourself. Repeat those positive statements aloud a few times. Keep this positive self-talk in mind as you write this week's manifestation statement.

Negative Talk   **Positive Spin**

....

....

....

....

....

....

....

....

....

....

....

....

369 Manifestations

In the morning, write what you want to manifest 3 times.

1. ....

2. ....

3. ....

In the afternoon, repeat what you want 6 times.

1. ....

2. ....

3. ....

4. ....

5. ....

6. ....

In the evening, reinforce your desires 9 times.

1. ....

2. ....

3. ....

4. ....

5. ....

6. ....

7. ....

8. ....

9. ....

Week 45

Schedule Your Goals

"Divide each difficulty into as many parts as is feasible and necessary to resolve it, and watch the whole transform."

—René Descartes

Time often slips away. We may resolve to act on our goals, but life has a way of throwing distractions at us until, before we know it, the week is over, and our task lists are still there with no items crossed off. One way to avoid this is to schedule a particular time to work on your goal. Make it like an appointment. Put it on your calendar. Tell household members that you've set that time aside. Put your phone on Do Not Disturb. If you have an office, shut the door. Isolate yourself for that period and work on your chosen task. If you can't finish during that time, set another appointment with yourself to continue. Try to make the micro-task you choose doable within your chosen time.

Exercise: Pick a task, write the action and your chosen time slot for working on it below, and put it on your calendar (paper, phone, or other). Set that time aside to work on that task and only that task. If an emergency comes up or it turns out to take longer, reschedule like you would an appointment and try again until you complete your chosen action.

Task

....

....

Date/Time

....

Task

....

....

Date/Time

....

Task

....

....

Date/Time

....

Task

....

....

Date/Time

....

369 Manifestations

In the morning, write what you want to manifest 3 times.

1. ....

2. ....

3. ....

In the afternoon, repeat what you want 6 times.

1. ....

2. ....

3. ....

4. ....

5. ....

6. ....

In the evening, reinforce your desires 9 times.

1. ....

2. ....

3. ....

4. ....

5. ....

6. ....

7. ....

8. ....

9. ....

Week 46

Motivate Yourself with Positive Affirmations

"The people who are crazy enough to think they can change the world are the ones who do."

—Steve Jobs

It's time to motivate yourself with positive affirmations, which can strengthen your sense of self and make you less defensive when exposed to information that might threaten your self-identity. This can make you more open-minded and less susceptible to misinformation.

Exercise: Create one to several positive affirmations, such as "I am an amazing human being" or "I have the skills I need to achieve my goals." Or, if you prefer, make them more detailed, personal, and relevant to your current goals. Repeat them several times aloud, on paper, or in your head. Keep this exercise in mind whenever you have a crisis of confidence. Feel free to repeat these affirmations every day, and as you write your weekly manifestation statement, know that you can do it!

I am...

I have...

369 Manifestations

In the morning, write what you want to manifest 3 times.

1. _____

2. _____

3. _____

In the afternoon, repeat what you want 6 times.

1. _____

2. _____

3. _____

4. _____

5. _____

6. _____

In the evening, reinforce your desires 9 times.

1. _____

2. _____

3. _____

4. _____

5. _____

6. _____

7. _____

8. _____

9. _____

Week 47

15 Minutes of Movement

"Not all those who wander are lost."

—J. R. R. Tolkien

Wandering around every now and then is good for you, physically and mentally. Get moving to improve your energy levels, decrease anxiety, improve mood, and spark your creativity, among many other benefits. Your physical and mental well-being are important to manifesting your desires and to leading a fulfilling life in general.

Exercise: Do the activity of your choice: tap dance, throw a ball against a wall, run around the yard with your dog—anything that gets you moving for fifteen minutes. Afterward, write down any ideas related to your manifestation goals—or anything else in your life—that spring to mind.

....

....

....

....

....

....

369 Manifestations

In the morning, write what you want to manifest 3 times.

1. ....

2. ....

3. ....

In the afternoon, repeat what you want 6 times.

1. ....

2. ....

3. ....

4. ....

5. ....

6. ....

In the evening, reinforce your desires 9 times.

1. ....

2. ....

3. ....

4. ....

5. ....

6. ....

7. ....

8. ....

9. ....

Write a Story

*"You can't use up creativity. The more
you use, the more you have."*

—Maya Angelou

It's once again time to exercise your creativity! The mind is an idea-generating machine. And imagination is something you don't run out of. Thoughts tend to branch off in many directions and spawn new ideas. Your unconscious mind even keeps working on things in your sleep. Have you ever gone to bed thinking about a project or problem and awoken with a related idea or even a solution? It happens!

Exercise: Use one of the following prompts to write a bit of micro-fiction or narrative nonfiction. Look at it again in the morning. Did any new ideas percolate overnight? Feel free to add to or revise the story before or after tackling this week's manifestation statement.

Prompts:

I remember that time when…

Macy heard a noise…

Leroy found cats to be curious creatures. This one…

369 Manifestations

In the morning, write what you want to manifest 3 times.

1.
2.
3.

In the afternoon, repeat what you want 6 times.

1.
2.
3.
4.
5.
6.

In the evening, reinforce your desires 9 times.

1.
2.
3.
4.
5.
6.
7.
8.
9.

Week 49

5-Minute Meditation

"The thing about meditation is you become more and more you."

—David Lynch, film maker

You can learn to practice mindfulness while doing almost anything, including sitting (see week 31). Sitting is something most of us do a lot. Why not use some of that sitting time to meditate? Just make sure you are in a comfortable position that you can hold for a few minutes. You can do whatever you like with your hands, including letting them dangle at your sides or rest on your lap. This meditation starts with the usual focus on breath and switches to focus on sounds. You can do it anywhere, even at the office.

Exercise: Do the following:

1. Write down how you feel on a line below.

2. Find a comfortable sitting position. It can be in a chair, on the floor, on a meditation stool, or wherever you find comfortable.

3. Focus on your breath as you breathe naturally. Notice the sensations it causes in the part of your body where you feel it most strongly.

4. Throughout the following steps, when your mind wanders, don't worry. This is normal. Just acknowledge the thoughts, dismiss them without self-criticism, and bring your attention back to the task at hand.

5. After a couple of minutes, switch your focus to your entire body and how it feels while breathing.

6. Next, switch your awareness to the sounds around you, internal and external—your stomach grumbling, the AC running, coworkers shuffling papers, birds chirping outside. Try to notice the sounds without thinking about what they are (i.e., don't think "That's the coffee machine," or "That's a bird," but rather note the volume and tone and other attributes of each sound).

7. Continue for five minutes or so.

8. Afterward, jot down how you feel again. Then, keep that pen or pencil moving as you write your weekly manifestation statement.

Before

....

....

....

....

After

....

....

....

....

369 Manifestations

In the morning, write what you want to manifest 3 times.

1. ....

2. ....

3. ....

In the afternoon, repeat what you want 6 times.

1. ....

2. ....

3. ....

4. ....

5. ....

6. ....

In the evening, reinforce your desires 9 times.

1. ....

2. ....

3. ....

4. ....

5. ....

6. ....

7. ....

8. ....

9. ....

Week 50

Give to Others

"Life's persistent and most urgent question is, 'What are you doing for others?'"

—Dr. Martin Luther King Jr.

Giving to others is good for the giver, the receiver, and society at large. As the old adage goes, give and you shall receive. Whether money, time, or action, give as much as you can. You won't regret it.

Exercise: Give something to a person, a group, or a cause: a gift, a donation, an act of activism, or some other sort of help or support. Jot down any feelings your act of generosity evoked. Then, write out your weekly manifestation statement with a generous heart.

369 Manifestations

In the morning, write what you want to manifest 3 times.

1. _____

2. _____

3. _____

In the afternoon, repeat what you want 6 times.

1. _____

2. _____

3. _____

4. _____

5. _____

6. _____

In the evening, reinforce your desires 9 times.

1. _____

2. _____

3. _____

4. _____

5. _____

6. _____

7. _____

8. _____

9. _____

Week 51

Acknowledge the Good

"Acknowledging the good that you already have in your life is the foundation for all abundance."

—Eckhart Tolle, spiritual teacher and self-help author

This is our last gratefulness exercise. But don't let that stop you! You can express gratefulness daily on your own—on paper, out loud, in your head, or even to other people. Keep up the practice to keep incurring the benefits.

What good things have happened lately? Have you reached any goals? Made any discoveries? Do you get to do fun things? Are there good people in your life? Again, coffee exists. And tea, if you aren't a java addict. You may even really enjoy water. We can all be grateful for a substance that keeps us alive.

Exercise: Think about and write down three or more things for which you are grateful. If you have more than three, bravo! Write all you can. Make it part of your regular routine! And remain grateful for all that you already have as you write this week's desired manifestation.

I'm grateful for

....

....

....

....

....

I'm grateful for

....

....

....

....

....

I'm grateful for

....

....

....

....

....

....

....

....

369 Manifestations

☀ In the morning, write what you want to manifest 3 times.

1. ....

2. ....

3. ....

☀ In the afternoon, repeat what you want 6 times.

1. ....

2. ....

3. ....

4. ....

5. ....

6. ....

☾ In the evening, reinforce your desires 9 times.

1. ....

2. ....

3. ....

4. ....

5. ....

6. ....

7. ....

8. ....

9. ....

Celebrate Your Achievements

"The significance of man is not in what he attains but in what he longs to attain."

—Kahlil Gibran

It's time to celebrate your accomplishments! Even if you haven't yet manifested all your desires, you put in an effort and got yourself on the path to doing so. Give yourself a round of applause. Reward yourself with a present, a night out, or something else you enjoy. Throw a party if you are so inclined. You deserve it.

Exercise: Brainstorm some things you'd like to do for yourself, pick one, and do it. Treat yourself! You've earned it.

Rewards

....

....

....

....

....

369 Manifestations

In the morning, write what you want to manifest 3 times.

1. ....

2. ....

3. ....

In the afternoon, repeat what you want 6 times.

1. ....

2. ....

3. ....

4. ....

5. ....

6. ....

In the evening, reinforce your desires 9 times.

1. ....

2. ....

3. ....

4. ....

5. ....

6. ....

7. ....

8. ....

9. ....

Conclusion,
But Not the End

You've come to the end of the journal and the beginning of the rest of your life. Hopefully you have gotten something out of this journey of reflection and self-improvement, manifested some desires, and discovered new ones in the process.

You can use this journal over and over. Repeat any techniques that worked for you and either jettison those that didn't or try them again to see what they yield. You can also try other versions of techniques and practices from this journal's exercises. For instance, if the mindfulness meditation exercises didn't seem to do anything for you, look into other types of meditation, of which there are many. You can also find alternate ways to perform self-affirmations, show gratitude, practice self-compassion, break large tasks down into smaller, more doable tasks, and so on. And there is no end to the ways you can feed your creativity and imagination. Read books, take courses, or take up art or music or writing, among many other possible creative activities.

The important thing is that you continue to believe in yourself and continue to work toward your desires with intention and positivity. You can do it!

References

"4 Proven Ways to Stimulate Your Imagination Throughout Your Day." *Mental Floss.* Accessed October 25, 2021. https://www.mentalfloss .com/article/517663/4-proven-ways-stimulate-your-imagination -throughout-your-day.

"7 Fun Exercises to Quickly Improve Creative Thinking." *Artwork Archive.* Accessed December 5, 2021. https://www.artworkarchive.com/blog/7- fun-exercises-to-quickly-improve-creative-thinking.

Ackerman, Courtney E. "22 Mindfulness Exercises, Techniques & Activities for Adults (+ PDF's)." PositivePsychology.com. Last updated December 13, 2021. https://positivepsychology.com/mindfulness -exercises-techniques-activities.

Ackerman, Courtney E. "What is Neuroplasticity: A Psychologist Explains [+14 Exercises]." PositivePsychology.com. Last updated February 5, 2022. https://positivepsychology.com/neuroplasticity.

Adams, A. J. "Seeing Is Believing: The Power of Visualization." *Psychology Today.* December 3, 2009. https://www.psychologytoday.com/us/blog /flourish/200912/seeing-is-believing-the-power-visualization.

Alidina, Shamash. *Mindfulness for Dummies.* Hoboken, New Jersey: John Wiley & Sons, Inc., 2020.

Andras, Simon. "7 Ways to Find Out What You Really Want in Life." *Lifehack.* Last updated February 4, 2021. https://www.lifehack.org /articles/communication/7-ways-find-out-what-you-really-want-life .html.

Ansorge, Rick. "Transcendental Meditation." WebMD. January 27, 2020. https://www.webmd.com/balance/guide/transcendental-meditation -benefits-technique.

Barringer, Daisy. "10 Exercises to Spark Original Thinking and Increase Creativity." Adobe. May 31, 2016. https://www.adobe.com/express /learn/blog/10-exercises-to-spark-original-thinking-and-unleash -creativity.

Borge, Jonathan. "40 Positive Affirmations to Add to Your Daily Rotation."
    Oprah Daily. May 19, 2021. https://www.oprahdaily.com/life
    /relationships-love/g25629970/positive-affirmations.

Boyles, Salynn. "Meditation May Reduce Pain." WebMD. April 6, 2011.
    https://www.webmd.com/balance/news/20110406/meditation-may
    -reduce-pain.

Byrne, Rhonda. *The Secret*. New York: Atria Books, 2007.

Canfield, Jack. "Visualization Techniques to Affirm Your Desired
    Outcomes: A Step-by-Step Guide." *Jack Canfield* (blog). https://www.
    jackcanfield.com/blog/visualize-and-affirm-your-desired-outcomes-a
    -step-by-step-guide.

Carter, Sherrie Bourg. "6 Reasons You Should Spend More Time Alone."
    Psychology Today. January 31, 2012. https://www.psychologytoday.com
    /us/blog/high-octane-women/201201/6-reasons-you-should-spend
    -more-time-alone.

Chandler, Nathan. "The Law of Attraction: Will the Universe Give You
    What You Want?" HowStuffWorks.com. Last updated April 8, 2021.
    https://people.howstuffworks.com/law-of-attraction.htm.

Chowdhury, Madhuleena Roy. "What Is Loving-Kindness Meditation?
    (Incl. 4 Scripts)." *Positive Psychology*. Last updated December 6, 2021.
    https://positivepsychology.com/loving-kindness-meditation.

Clarke, Christopher Lloyd. "How to Write Affirmations That Really
    Work!" The Guided Meditation Site. Accessed September 19, 2021.
    https://www.the-guided-meditation-site.com/how-to-write
    -affirmations.html.

"Cognitive Restructuring: Socratic Questions." Therapist Aid. Accessed
    October 30, 2021. https://www.therapistaid.com/therapy-worksheet
    /socratic-questioning/cbt/none.

Davis, Tchiki. "How to Manifest Something (Manifest Love, Money, or
    Anything.)." Berkeley Well-Being Institute. https://www
    .berkeleywellbeing.com/how-to-manifest.html.

Editors of the Encyclopaedia Britannica. "Numerology." *Britannica*.
    January 16, 2018. https://www.britannica.com/topic/numerology.

Entrepreneurs' Organization. "How to Apply the Law of Attraction in
    Business: 5 Steps." *Inc.* August 7, 2018. https://www.inc.com
    /entrepreneurs-organization/how-to-apply-law-of-attraction-in
    -business-5-steps.html.

Gaines, Jeffrey. "Fostering Creativity: 12 Tips for Boosting Your Creative Skills." *Positive Psychology*. Last updated August 30, 2021. https://positivepsychology.com/creativity.

Gill, Bhali. "New to Visualization? Here Are 5 Steps to Get You Started." *Forbes*. June 22, 2017. https://www.forbes.com/sites /bhaligill/2017/06/22/new-to-visualization-here-are-5-steps-to-get -you-started.

Globokar, Lidija. "The Power of Visualization and How to Use It." *Forbes*. March 5, 2020. https://www.forbes.com/sites/lidijaglobokar/2020 /03/05/the-power-of-visualization-and-how-to-use-it.

Goldsmith, Barton. "How to Believe in Yourself More." *Psychology Today*. October 20, 2021. https://www.psychologytoday.com/us/blog /emotional-fitness/202110/how-believe-in-yourself-more.

Graebner, Kerstin. "How to Practice Self Compassion and Tame Your Inner Critic." *BetterUp*. June 18, 2021. https://www.betterup.com/blog /self-compassion.

Groth, Aimee, and Ashley Lutz. "12 Ways the 'Law of Attraction' Can Improve Your Life." *Business Insider*. July 31, 2012. https://www.businessinsider.com/how-the-law-of-attraction-will -improve-your-life-2012-7.

Grubin, David. *The American Experience*. Season 28, Episode 7, "Tesla." Aired October 18, 2016, PBS. Amazon Prime.

Gulino, Elizabeth. "The 369 Manifestation Method Is Going Viral on TikTok. Here's How To Do It." *Refinery29*. Last updated January 12, 2021. https://www.refinery29.com/en-us/369-manifestation-method -how-to-do.

Haanel, Charles F. *The Master Key System*. Read by Michael A. Harding. Cromes Publishing Audio, 2020. 7 hours, 8 minutes.

"How to Do the 369 Manifestation Method." *The Manifestation Collective* (blog). January 7, 2021. https://themanifestationcollective.co/369 -manifestation-method.

Jabr, Ferris. "Why Walking Helps Us Think." *The New Yorker*. September 3, 2014. https://www.newyorker.com/tech/annals-of-technology/walking -helps-us-think.

Khoshaba, Deborah. "A Seven-Step Prescription for Self-Love." *Psychology Today*. March 27, 2012. https://www.psychologytoday.com/us/blog/get -hardy/201203/seven-step-prescription-self-love.

LaCapria, Kim. "Nikola Tesla '369 Theory.'" TruthorFiction.com. August 3, 2021. https://www.truthorfiction.com/nikola-tesla-369-theory.

Lively, Kathryn J. "Affirmations: The Why, What, How, and What If?" *Psychology Today*. March 12, 2014. https://www.psychologytoday.com /us/blog/smart-relationships/201403/affirmations-the-why-what-how -and-what-if.

Mayo Clinic Staff. "Exercise: 7 Benefits of Regular Physical Activity." Mayo Clinic. October 8, 2021. https://www.mayoclinic.org/healthy-lifestyle /fitness/in-depth/exercise/art-20048389.

McGreevey, Sue. "Eight Weeks to a Better Brain." *Harvard Gazette*. January 21, 2011. https://news.harvard.edu/gazette/story/2011/01 /eight-weeks-to-a-better-brain.

Miller, Kori D. "14 Health Benefits of Practicing Gratitude According to Science." *Positive Psychology*. Last updated February 14, 2022. https://positivepsychology.com/benefits-of-gratitude.

Moore, Catherine. "Positive Daily Affirmations: Is There Science Behind It?" *Positive Psychology*. Last updated February 4, 2022. https://positivepsychology.com/daily-affirmations.

Morin, Amy. "7 Scientifically Proven Benefits of Gratitude." *Psychology Today*. April 3, 2015. https://www.psychologytoday.com/us/blog /what-mentally-strong-people-dont-do/201504/7-scientifically-proven -benefits-gratitude.

Novotney, Amy. "The Science of Creativity." *gradPSYCH* Magazine. 2009. https://www.apa.org/gradpsych/2009/01/creativity#.

O'Neill, Barbara. "Strategies to Take Positive Action." Rutgers.edu. August 2015. https://njaes.rutgers.edu/sshw/message/message .php?p=Finance&m=305.

Patel, Deep. "8 Ways to Stay Accountable With Your Goals." *Entrepreneur*. March 6, 2019. https://www.entrepreneur.com/article/328070.

Patel, Deep. "16 Actions to Take to Achieve Any Goal." *Entrepreneur*. August 27, 2018. https://www.entrepreneur.com/article/318347.

"Positive Psychology: Practicing the Power of Positive Thinking." *U.S. Preventative Medicine*. August 1, 2017. https://www.uspm.com /practice-the-power-of-positive-thinking.

"Practicing Gratitude Works." CDC.gov. Last updated April 16, 2021. https://www.cdc.gov/howrightnow/gratitude/index.html.

"Relaxation techniques: Breath Control Helps Quell Errant Stress Response." Harvard Medical School. July 6, 2020. https://www.health .harvard.edu /mind-and-mood/relaxation-techniques-breath-control-helps-quell -errant-stress-response.

Reynolds, Gretchen. "Can Exercise Make You More Creative?" *New York Times*. Last updated February 5, 2021. https://www.nytimes .com/2021/02/03/well/exercise-creativity.html.

Riopel, Leslie. "26 Mental Heath Exercises and Interventions Based on Science." *Positive Psychology*. Last updated December 13, 2021. https://positivepsychology.com/mental-health-exercises-interventions/.

Riopel, Leslie. "30 Meditation Exercises and Activities to Practice Today." *Positive Psychology*. Last updated February 4, 2022. https://positivepsychology.com/meditation-exercises-activities.

Robson, David. "Why Self-Compassion—Not Self-Esteem—Leads to Success." BBC. January 13, 2021. https://www.bbc.com/worklife /article/20210111-why-self-compassion-not-self-esteem-leads-to -success.

Savin, Jennifer. "What Is the 369 Manifestation Method That's Blowing Up on Tiktok?" *Cosmopolitan*. March 30, 2021. https://www.cosmopolitan .com/uk/body/health/a35965423/369-manifestation-method-tiktok.

Schultz, Joshua. "5 Differences Between Mindfulness and Meditation." *Positive Psychology*. Last updated February 5, 2022. https:// positivepsychology.com/differences-between-mindfulness-meditation.

Segerstrom, Suzanne. "The Structure and Consequences of Repetitive Thought." American Psychological Association. March 2011. https://www.apa.org/science/about/psa/2011/03/repetitive-thought.

Sites, Betsi, and Tchiki Davis. "Positive Affirmations: Definition, Examples, and Exercises." Berkeley Well-Being Institute. https://www .berkeleywellbeing.com/positive-affirmations.html.

Suttie, Jill, and Jason Marsh. "5 Ways Giving Is Good for You." *Greater Good Magazine*. December 13, 2010. https://greatergood.berkeley.edu /article/item/5_ways_giving_is_good_for_you.

Sutton, Jeremy. "Socratic Questioning in Psychology: Examples and Techniques." *Positive Psychology*. February 7, 2022. https:// positivepsychology.com/socratic-questioning.

Swart, Tara. "This Is a Visualization Exercise That Actually Works, According To Neuroscience." *Fast Company*. May 9, 2019. https://www.fastcompany.com/90346545/this-is-a-visualization-exercise-that-actually-works-according-to-neuroscience.

Tesla, Nikola. *My Inventions: The Autobiography of Nikola Tesla*. Read by Ron Welch. 2017. Audible audio ed, 2 hours, 53 minutes.

Travis, Abi. "TikTok Users Claim They Changed Their Lives Using the '3 6 9 Manifestation Method.'" *Distractify*. Last updated June 22, 2020. https://www.distractify.com/p/3-6-9-manifestation-method-tiktok.

Vilhauer, Jennice. "How to Figure Out What You Want in Life." *Psychology Today*. September 30, 2019. https://www.psychologytoday.com/us/blog/living-forward/201909/how-figure-out-what-you-want-in-life.

Villarica, Hans. "How the Power of Positive Thinking Won Scientific Credibility." *The Atlantic*. April 23, 2012. https://www.theatlantic.com/health/archive/2012/04/how-the-power-of-positive-thinking-won-scientific-credibility/256223.

"Visualize Your Goals." Tony Robbins (blog). https://www.tonyrobbins.com/how-to-focus/goal-visualization.

"Walking Meditation." *Greater Good in Action*. https://ggia.berkeley.edu/practice/walking_meditation.

"Walking Meditation Guide: How to Meditate While Walking." MasterClass.com. Last updated March 3, 2021. https://www.masterclass.com/articles/walking-meditation-guide#what-is-walking-meditation.

Wilson Jr., Robert Evans. "Exercise Your Imagination NOW!" *Psychology Today*. September 10, 2018. https://www.psychologytoday.com/us/blog/the-main-ingredient/201809/exercise-your-imagination-now.

Wilson Jr., Robert Evans. "Four Easy Ways to Exercise Your Creativity." *Psychology Today*. June 14, 2016. https://www.psychologytoday.com/us/blog/the-main-ingredient/201606/four-easy-ways-exercise-your-creativity.

Acknowledgments

I am grateful for all my loved ones, who make my life's journey well worth it, wherever it may lead.

I am grateful for the experts who have studied the effects of the positive practices within this journal, and the practitioners who have shared their knowledge with the world. Researching this book has been a joy that has changed me for the better.

And I am very grateful for Renee Rutledge, Kierra Sondereker, Claire Chun, Raquel Castro, Yesenia Garcia Lopez, Barbara Schultz, and all the others at Ulysses Press who worked hard to bring this journal to fruition. I can't wait to see the finished product and use it myself!

About the Author

Berni Johnson is a writer, IT worker, and lifelong learner interested in everything from the inner workings of the mind to the outer workings of the entire physical universe. She has spent the last few decades looking into ways to quell the anxiety she seems to have been born with and thinks she finally has a handle on it.

You can find Berni's blog, social media links, and links to her fiction and nonfiction books, articles, and stories at www.bernijohnson.com.